FEARLESS

How to Conquer Fear Forever

GREGORY DICKOW

Fearless: How to Conquer Fear Forever
©2015 by Gregory Dickow Ministries.

All rights reserved.

Unless otherwise noted, all Scripture quotations in this volume are from the King James Version of the Bible.

Scripture quotations marked (AMP) are taken from the Amplified Bible, Copyright © 1954, 1958, 1962, 1964, 1965, 1987 by The Lockman Foundation.
Used by permission.

Printed in the United States of America

For information, please write
Gregory Dickow Ministries,
P.O. Box 7000
Chicago, IL 60680

or visit us online at www.gregorydickow.org.

ISBN 13: 978-1-932833-26-3

First Printing 2015

TABLE OF CONTENTS

FEARLESS

Introduction

Fear is at the root of just about every negative thing that happens in our lives. We're afraid of failing, being alone, or rejection; afraid of running out of money; afraid that people will let us down; afraid that we won't find a spouse, or the one we found will leave us (or in some cases that they WON'T leave us—ha, ha!). We're afraid something bad may happen to us or our children—and the list goes on and on.

All fear is rooted in the core belief that God's Word won't work. For example, the fear of not having enough is rooted in the fear that Philippians 4:19 isn't true. If you believe that "God will supply all your needs according to His riches, . . ." then fear leaves. There is a promise from God's Word for every need you will ever have. In fact, there are over 7,000 promises in the Bible. That's 7,000 solutions to overcome fear! 1 John 4:18 says, "Perfect love casts out fear." What a comforting promise! Although we're certainly not perfect, God's divine love for us IS perfect! If He would die for you while you were in sin, separated from God, there's just nothing He wouldn't do for you!

As you dive into this book, your mind will be flooded with thoughts of God's Word and His love, driving fear far from your life forever!

Get ready to become absolutely FEARLESS!

Chapter One
PERFECT LOVE
CASTS OUT FEAR

"As He is, so are we in this world."

1 John 4:17

Although we are all full of flaws and shortcomings, God just doesn't see us that way! He sees us just as He sees Jesus. Jesus was the firstborn of many brethren (Romans 8:29). The moment we are born again, we are the brethren He was the first-born of! To God, you are like Jesus' twin brother or sister! He loves you the same. He sees you the same! How we view ourselves, however, is what needs to change; because how we see ourselves on the inside is how we will ultimately live on the outside.

God doesn't look at you based on your performance. This is hard to accept when you've lived your life based on a performance mentality. When you realize God's approval and affection for you, then it frees you to *want* to obey God rather than having to obey God.

Love is the root to our relationship with God. Song of Solomon 1:2 says, "Let him kiss me over and over again with the kisses of His mouth! Your love is better than wine." That's the kind of relationship that God wants to have with you and me!

Just as honeymoon couples can't stop expressing their love to each other, that's how God is toward us continually.

Christianity is a love affair with God. When you're in love with someone, and they're in love with you, there's no fear that they're going to leave you, judge you, or fail to provide for you. When the loving feelings wear off, we begin to question, and fear creeps in. Fear comes when we're not in love anymore. But that is human love: the love of the lovely, the attractive, the beautiful.

But God's divine love is not like that. God loves us because He IS love.

God doesn't love us because we are lovely. In fact, we are often anything but lovely! He doesn't love us because of something we've done. And He doesn't judge us because of something we haven't done. We have to understand the nature of God. He is GOOD—all the time! God doesn't take life; He gives life. God doesn't hurt, He heals. The life of Jesus is the picture of God's love for us. Jesus never takes healing away; He gives healing. He doesn't take sight away; He gives sight. He doesn't withhold food; He multiplies it!

1 John 4:18—"There is no fear in love; but perfect love banishes all fear."

What is this perfect love that banishes all fear?

Perfect love is love that you can't stop. There's nothing you can do to gain it. And there's nothing you can do to lose it. God's love is free. It's nothing you can work for, earn, or deserve. Perfect love is *telios agape,* in Greek, which means total and complete unmerited love. There's nothing you can do to add to it or take away from it, because it's based on God's character and His promises, not our character or our promises.

The Prodigal Son and Father: A Picture of Perfect Love.

In Luke 15, the prodigal son wastes away his inheritance with selfish living. When he comes to his senses, he says, *"I will arise and go to my Father"* (verses 17–18). This represents the perfect will of God for our lives. When we realize we can get up when we've fallen and "arise and go to our Father," we are headed toward God's perfect will. An understanding of God's perfect love, brings us into God's perfect will.

"And while he was yet a great way off, his father saw him" (Luke 15:20). We all have been a great way off—away from God, outside of His will, having fallen short many times. This son was WAY OFF, and yet the Father saw him and had compassion on him. The father ran to his son (Luke 15:20). That's a picture of how God is toward us. Even when we are way off, far from God and far from His will for our lives, He comes running to us! He puts His arms around us, in our filth and shame. He embraces and kisses us continually with the kisses of His love.

As we continue to study this story of the prodigal son, let me show you seven major fears each of us have and how the kisses of our Heavenly Father will sweep all those fears away.

1. The fear of rejection. "Maybe he'll rebuke me or remind me of my past," the son might have thought. The father puts his arm around his son and falls on his neck. This is total acceptance. He kissed him. The literal translation is, "He continued to kiss him." The kiss of acceptance delivers us from rejection.

2. The fear of judgment. "Maybe he will judge or condemn me," the son might have thought. But this continual kissing meant that all was forgiven. The kiss of forgiveness delivers us from the fear of judgment.

3. The fear of loss. The son wants to come back as a servant, but the father's kisses mean, "I restore you as a son. You're not a slave. Your privileges are restored!" This delivers us from the fear of loss.

4. The fear of the curse and lack. The father's kiss represents the blessing in our lives. "I bless you. I don't curse you. I will not leave you in the condition I found you. You will not remain in this cycle of defeat and failure. You're blessed, not cursed!" This delivers us from the fear of lack.

5. The fear of being lonely, or depressed. The father's kisses say, "You probably feel depressed, lonely, left out, like an outcast, but I am with you. You're not alone anymore!" This is the kiss of comfort and companionship.

6. The fear that things are going to be taken away. The continual kisses mean, "My love for you is real. I reassure you I'm not going to turn on you. You haven't lost your sonship, just because you lost your way. I'm here to give, not to take away."

7. The fear of disapproval. When the older brother disapproves of celebrating the lost son's return, the father reaffirms his approval of his son's return. Often our own fellow believers won't approve of us; but God still does, even when we've failed.

What do we have to do? Nothing, except to *come to our senses* about what God is really like. He LOVES us!

We often think we have to clean ourselves up, but this son was in filth when his father kissed him. This father kissed his son because he loved him. The father did the running, the kissing, the restoring, and the blessing. You know what changed this son? The father's unconditional love. What will change you? This same unconditional love. Revelation 1:5–6 says, ". . . He loved us, He washed us, then He made us kings and priests." Notice, God doesn't love what was washed. He washed what He loved. He loved us first! Then washed us. Then made us kings and priests!

Chapter One Summary

God doesn't look at us based on our performance, flaws, or shortcomings. When He sees us, He sees Jesus. God loves us with divine love and His perfect love casts out fear. God is love and His love is complete: nothing can be done to add to or take away from it. The continual kisses of the father to the prodigal son show us how perfect love casts out all of our fears.

Scripture References: 1 John 4:17–18, Romans 8:29, Luke 15:17–20

Chapter Two
WHEN GOD SAYS:
I LOVE YOU!

Perfect love drives out fear.

1 John 4:18

We live in a fearful world and generation. When you awaken to God's perfect love towards you, it casts all the fear from your life. You don't have to drive it out. Love does.

God's love isn't based on what we can do, because it's His love—it's perfect.

If you're always performing to please people or receive their love or approval, you'll always be operating in the fear that perhaps you won't receive their approval if you don't perform well enough. But there's just nothing we can do to earn or lose God's approval.

God's love is perfect for three reasons. When God says, "I love you," He means three things:

1. "I'll never break My promise to you." God bases His promises on His love, not on how we perform. Love is an unbreakable promise from God. Don't think of it in terms of, "How can I get God to keep His word?" Simply accept that He will keep His promise because He is good. He is God. And He is love! All we have to do is focus on His goodness and love, then fear will leave. For example, 2 Timothy 2:13 tells us, "Even when we are faithless, He remains faithful, for He cannot deny Himself." This delivers us from the mindset that it's all up to us. We don't need great faith—just faith in a great God. God's love is unconditional. His promise is based on His love, not ours. It's not up to us, because if it were, none of us could earn it. God keeping His promise doesn't have to do with us being holy enough. It has to do with Him being holy enough.

2. "I will never leave you or forsake you." This casts out the fear of being alone or lonely. He will never leave you out or cast you out. Today's culture seems to have what I like to call, *Dixie cup love.* This is where people treat others and relationships as if they are disposable. God is not like that! In the book of Hosea, God tells a prophet to love a harlot—even when she returns to her harlotry! God will heal the backslider. Did she deserve to be forsaken? Yes. Do we deserve to be forsaken? Yes. But He will never leave us or forsake us! That makes me love Him even more! God doesn't want us to love Him because we have to. I love Him and follow Him because He is the most wonderful Being in the universe. He is the most loving, forgiving, merciful, and affectionate Being in the universe. Without Him, where would we be?

3. "I will never remember your past."

God doesn't remember our past. He doesn't cover it. He washes it away. We've all had a fear that our past will be brought up. But God's love casts out that fear. "And your sins & your iniquities, I will remember NO MORE" (Hebrews 8:12).

Chapter Two Summary

God's love toward us is perfect, divine love. Divine love casts out fear, because there's nothing we can do to make Him love us more or less. God doesn't need us, but He wants us because He loves us. God's love is perfect for three reasons: When God says He loves you, He means, "I'll never break my promise to you," "I'll never leave or forsake you," and "I'll never remember

your past."

Scripture References: 1 John 4:18,

Hosea 1:2, Hebrews 8:12

Chapter Three
THE PROBLEM IS
NOT THE PROBLEM

God spoke to me some time ago and said, "Tell my people I have prepared them for the storms they're about to face. I have prepared them for EVERY storm they will ever face." And it's His love that prepares us for the storms, so that we don't have to fear whatever comes our way. It's my hope that this simple book is giving you something today that will prepare you for tomorrow's storm.

Fear Not.

It's time that we obliterate the power and force of fear. The Gospel is a message of: FEAR NOT. The moment we accept Jesus as Lord, we're delivered instantly from judgment and the fear that comes from it.

The problem is not the problem.

The problems in our lives are not the real problem. We do things that deal with the surface but not the root of a problem. For example, many medications cover the symptoms, dealing with the effect and not the cause. In marriage, we can tend to focus on a little surface issue. How your spouse squeezes the toothpaste tube or doesn't put the cap back on is not the real issue!

Let me try to show you what I mean:

Mark 4:35–41: On the same day, when evening had come, He said to them, "Let us cross over to the other side." Now when they had left the multitude, they took Him along in the boat as He was . . . And a great windstorm arose, and the waves beat into the boat, so that it was already filling. But He was in the stern, asleep on a pillow. And they awoke Him and said to Him, "Teacher, do You not care that we are perishing?" Then He arose and rebuked the wind, and said to the sea, "Peace, be still!" And the wind ceased and there was a great calm. But He said to them, "Why are you so fearful? How is it that you have no faith?" And they feared exceedingly, and said to one another, "Who can this be, that even the wind and the sea obey Him!"

The passage of the storm in Mark 4:35–41 occurred the very SAME DAY that Jesus said earlier, "The sower sows the Word"

(Mark 4:14), and "The Kingdom of God is like a man who casts seed in the ground and goes to sleep" (Mark 4:26). Here, Jesus sums up the Kingdom of God: 1. The man plants seed; 2. He goes to sleep; 3. The seed grows.

Now notice this: "On the same day, when evening had come, He said to them, "Let us cross over to the other side" (Mark 4:35). Here we see Jesus has planted the seed of God's Word. In essence, He is promising, "We are going to the other side!"

He's planting the seed. When the storm hits, He is at peace. In fact, He is asleep. There is a storm filling their boat, but Jesus is sleeping! Most of us want step two in the face of the storm—we want peace. We want sleep. But we often skip step one: plant the seed.

You see, the storm was not the problem. If it were, Jesus would not have slept through it. The goal in life is not to get rid of all our problems and storms; but to simply get through them without harm. Jesus said, pray this way: "Give us this day our daily bread." In other words, "Give us what we're going to need at the beginning of the day so we're prepared for whatever comes our way."

The storm simply revealed the problem that already existed.

The problem was that the disciples were ruled by the storm, resulting in fear rather than being ruled by God's love and promises. When Jesus said, "Let us go to the other side," He was making a promise: that they would make it to the other side! God's promises don't deny that problems will exist, but God's promises deny them the power to control our lives! We have to stop living our lives, running from our problems or even running around to try to put out all the fires of our problems. Don't give your problem that much power over you! If we're chasing all the fires around us to put them all out, then the fires and problems of life are leading us. Instead, just walk through the fire; and you will not be burned! Just worship in the midst of the problem, and the devil will realize he can't control you anymore!

The problem was not the storm; the storm revealed the problem. What this really revealed here was that the disciples didn't believe the promise of Jesus. He wasn't yet the promise keeper to them. He was just a good teacher. You see, when the storm hit, "They awoke Him and said to Him, '*Teacher,* do You not care that we are perishing?'" (Mark 4:38) Fear was now their master. Jesus was just their *teacher*!

"Don't you care?" This question implies wrong assumptions about God. When we get afraid, we start blaming

God or accusing Him of not caring. This fear often makes us angry. Fear is the root to second-guessing God. Fear makes us forget what we already have going for us. Fear attacked the disciples' relationship with God. They forgot what already belonged to them in the midst of the storm.

Here is the secret: Whenever fear comes, take inventory of what you have. God's love never leaves us empty handed. His love is always accompanied with a gift! And in this case, He armed them with four powerful gifts

to make it through the storm. And He has armed YOU with these same four powerful gifts:

1. The disciples had a promise. Jesus said, *"We're going to the other side."* Start your day, business, family, marriage, with a promise from God. God has given us 7,000 promises. And unlike socks and underwear, you can use the same ones over and over every day! If you face a storm without a promise, that storm will beat you. Face it with a promise: it's unbreakable. **God always prepares you for a storm—with a promise.**

2. They had God's presence. Sometimes we forget He is with us. "Though I walk through the valley of the shadow of death, I will fear no evil. Because Thou art with me" (Psalm 23:4). Somehow, some way, that promise is going to come to pass, because the promise keeper is with us!

3. They had power. They could have spoken to the storm. We're constantly trying to wake God up, when we really should be waking up His power within ourselves. Wake your tongue up and speak God's Word to your storm!

4. They had God's purpose. God's purpose is always greater than the problem. Declare this in the midst of your storm: "This storm is not going to drown or defeat me because I haven't fulfilled His complete purpose for my life yet. I shall live and not die and declare the works of the Lord! According to Jeremiah 29:11, God's plans for me are good and not evil. If this storm defeats me, that would be evil. So I say to the storm, 'Peace, be still!'"

Now when the next problem comes, you know how to deal with it because you've learned the problem is not the problem. And you have taken inventory of what you ALREADY have!

Jesus calmed the storm. Why? The only one who can calm the storm is the one who is not afraid of it. You can't speak to a mountain and make it move when you're afraid of it. Jesus commanded the storm, because He wasn't commanded by it. Don't react to the storms in your life. When you're afraid, find a promise. The Word is God's love letter to you. Rest in His promise. Rest in His love; and when something starts troubling you, speak to it. It is not your problem; fear is. And God's promises are the proof of His love. He is watching over His Word to perform it. Don't worry and don't be afraid. It will come to pass because God is a covenant-keeping God.

Chapter Three Summary:

The storm in the fourth chapter of Mark did not wake Jesus. The disciples said, "Teacher, don't you care that we'll perish?" But Jesus was resting on the pillow of God's love (verses 37–38). Psalm 127:1 says, "He gives to His beloved in their sleep." Jesus was sleeping on the pillow of God's love. When you go to sleep you can accept what I call His "love me while I'm sleepin' love."

We are delivered from fear because God prepares us for every trial we will ever face. We can make it through any problem, trial or temptation when we realize we have four powerful gifts. Never forget that whenever you go through a storm, you have His promise, His presence, His power, and His purpose.

Scripture References: Mark 4:35–41, Mark 4:14, Mark 4:26, Jeremiah 29:11, Psalm 127:2

Chapter Four

THE POWER TO BE FREE FROM FEAR FOREVER!

Let us again first read and internalize our powerful key passage from God's Word to solidify in our minds and hearts, once and forever: that it's His amazing love that frees us from all fear!

1 John 4:16–18: "And we have known and believed the love that God has for us. God is love; and he that abides in love abides in God, and God in Him. Herein is our love made perfect, that we may have boldness in the day of judgment: because as He is, so are we in this world. There is no fear in love; but perfect love casts out fear: because **fear hath torment**… "

"WHY DOES FEAR HAVE TORMENT?"

I asked this question of the Lord a while back, and here's what I believe He showed me: "Fear has torment because it paralyzes My people. It keeps them stuck and I don't want my people stuck."

In this chapter, we are going to look at some of the ways fear stops us from going forward, and we will banish these fears forever.

1. Fear gets us comparing ourselves to others. We won't be happy when we compare ourselves to others and to what they have. We can only be second-best at being someone else! Besides, God has a special portion reserved just for you, so you don't have to be afraid of missing out! The Bible tells us in 2 Corinthians 10:12, "When we compare ourselves to others, we are without understanding."

2. Fear makes us think we could never change. Perhaps you've feared that you'll always be the same, never able to overcome. But beloved, "be confident of this very thing, that He who has begun a good work in you WILL complete it!" (Philippians 1:6)

3. Fear makes us afraid that we will not have what we want. God is not holding any good thing back from us. Psalm 84:11 says, "No good things does He withhold from the righteous." Well, you and I are the righteousness of God, the moment we accept Jesus Christ as our Savior and Lord. So, since we are now righteous, He will not withhold any good thing from us. There is nothing to fear when you realize that, "He who did not spare His own Son, but delivered Him up for us all, how shall He not also, WITH HIM, freely give us all things" (Romans 8:32).

Wow! There is nothing to fear when you realize He isn't holding anything back from you. That was the trick serpent used to get Adam and Eve to sin. When he got them to believe that God was holding out on them, it awakened in them a lust for what they shouldn't have. They lost focus on ALL the trees that God told them they could freely eat from. Had they focused on ALL that He had given them, they wouldn't have been focused at all on the tree that He told them not to eat from. Every time we believe the lie that God is holding out on us, we will always try to obtain things for ourselves as an act of self-preservation. But when we realize He has provided EVERY good tree for us to eat FREELY from, we lose our appetite for the lust of the flesh, the lust of the eyes, and the pride of life.

4. Fear is a magnet for failure in our lives. Fear is a force that causes the very thing we're afraid of to come to pass. We find this truth in Job 3:25. Job said, "What I have feared, has come upon me."

For example, if you're afraid nobody is going to like you, you'll probably give off that impression to others—projecting to them the fear that they don't like you. People can pick up on that and as a result, reject you— not because of you, but because of the fear.

5. Fear gets us to doubt that God's Word will work. All fear is the result of not believing a promise from God. For example, if I'm afraid of not having enough food or money, it's because I don't believe Philippians 4:19—that God shall supply all my need.

Or fear makes us think that the pain we're going through will never stop. Let us remember and believe Jesus bore our pains on His body and carried them away on the cross! (Isaiah 53:4)

HOW TO BE FREE FROM FEAR:

Are you ready for your breakthrough?!

This verse will set you free…

"God has not given us a spirit of fear, but of power, love and a sound mind" (2 Timothy 1:7).

Notice the three gifts God gives, and how they can free us from fear:

1. Power. Power delivers us from fear, because all fear comes from a sense of powerlessness over our situation. When we feel powerless over past, present, or future circumstances, we become afraid. Fear begins to be pushed out when we discover we have the power to do something about our lives. What kind of power do we have?

- We have power over our future through the seeds we sow. If you plant corn seed, you can have confidence that your future contains stalks of corn!

- We have power over our past through the blood of Jesus. He has removed and forgotten our past sins and failures (Psalm 103:12, Hebrews 8:12).

- We have power over our present condition, with the words we speak— Mark 11:23. Death and life are in the power of the tongue (Proverbs 18:21).

- We have power over the devil, demons and all the forces of darkness (Luke 10:19, 2 Corinthians 10:3–5).

- We have power in prayer! (James 5:17)

2. A Sound Mind. This means to think from God's point of view as expressed in His Word. The word, sound, means 'whole'. A person with a sound mind comes into agreement with God's way of seeing and thinking. Fear starts with incomplete information. When we don't see the whole picture—from God's point of view—we will become afraid. When Elisha's servant only saw the enemy around him, he became afraid. So Elisha asked God to "open his eyes," and THEN he saw that there were more for him than those against him—2 Kings 6:16–17. When he SAW the whole picture, fear left! That's a SOUND mind!

3. Love. 1 John 4:10 says, "This is love, not that we loved God, but that He loved us, and sent His Son to be the substitute for our sins." When you understand perfect love, it delivers you from fear. And perfect love is that He first loved us! Think about it: we only love Him back. Love didn't start with us. He so perfectly loved us that He would send us His Son in the midst of all our weaknesses and shortcomings. That's the kind of love that drives out all fear. We never have to fear that He will leave us when we fall, because He saved us while we were completely fallen!

IT'S TIME TO BE BOLD!

Remember, "Herein is our love made perfect, that we may have boldness in the day of judgment: because as He is, so are we in this world" (1 John 4:17).

When is the day of judgment that this verse is speaking of? Is it when we die and go to heaven? No, because we won't need boldness then. He is talking about while we are "in this world." We can have boldness when the devil tries to judge us, when our past tries to judge us, or when others try to judge us—that's the day of judgment! You are the righteousness of God, so you can stand in God's presence with confidence, no matter what tries to judge or condemn you. God has accepted you. You can go boldly to the throne of His grace and receive! (Hebrews 4:16.) When you realize this, there is no reason left to fear.

What gives us this bold confidence?

When we know who we are, boldness comes. "The wicked flee when no one is pursuing, but the righteous are as bold as a lion" (Proverbs 28:1). The lion knows he's the king of the jungle. You might think you are like a little kitty cat, but you are made of the royal blood of Jesus Christ! Jesus is the lion of the tribe of Judah (Revelation 5:5). Inside of you is lion's blood! When you know who you are, you can be fearless to get back up, no matter how far you've fallen or how beaten down you are. According to Revelation 1:6, you are a king and a priest! You can speak to sickness, fear, or sin, and it will obey you and flee!

Chapter Four Summary

God has not given us a spirit of fear. Fear comes from a sense of powerlessness, but we are free from fear when we understand the three amazing gifts God has given us: power, love and a sound mind! We become fearless in our thinking when we see things from God's point of view, when we realize how much power we have, and when we realize how loved we are! So you can be bold in the face of fear, because the righteous are as bold as a lion. Have confidence in knowing who you are, like the lion, who knows he's the king of the jungle. Inside of you is the Lion of the Tribe of Judah. And as He is in this world, so are we—FEARLESS!

Scripture References: 2 Timothy 1:7, 1 John 4:10, 16–18, Proverbs 28:1

FEARLESS

Concluding Thoughts

Beloved, with this new revelation of God's perfect love for you and new understanding of who you really are, you are prepared to stand fearless in the face of any fear that tries to creep into your life, mind, or emotions. You can cast it out with the boldness of a lion!

Remember, God's Word is true, whether you feel it or not. He has kept all of His promises for 6,000 years of human history and has never failed. Fear will leave you when you rely on something that can't fail: the promises of God! (2 Corinthians 1:20.)

When God says, "I love you," He means that He will NEVER break His promises to you! God has made 7,000 promises to you in the Bible to prepare you for anything and everything that will ever come your way. And one of the greatest promises of all is this: "Yea, though I walk through the valley of the shadow of death, I will fear no evil, for You are with me!" (Psalm 23:4)

Declare this out loud today: *I will never live in fear another day of my life, because God has not given me a spirit of fear, but of power, love, and a sound mind! God has perfect love toward me, which banishes all fear. He loves me because He loves me—not because of what I have done or can do. He is my Father and comes running to me whenever I fall. He has made me His son or daughter! I am His, and He is mine. He kisses me with the kisses of His unconditional love and acceptance, and they sweep away all my fears. He is watching*

over His Word to perform it, and He will
not break any of His good promises toward
me. What a loving God! What an amazing
Father! What a beautiful Savior I have, in
Jesus' Name! AMEN!

Receive the Gift of Salvation

Perhaps you have never received Jesus
Christ as your Savior and Lord, or you're not
sure you will go to heaven when you die.
Well, you can be sure today. Or perhaps
you have tried to be good, and you thought,
"If I am good enough, if I go to church or try

to clean up my life, then I will be saved." But none of that will save you. There is only one way to go to heaven—by accepting forgiveness and the gift of salvation, through the sacrifice Jesus made on the Cross. I want to lead you in this prayer of faith, and something miraculous is going to happen in your heart. Pray this out loud:

"Heavenly Father, I accept Jesus Christ into my life as my Lord and as my Savior. I believe Jesus died for my sins and rose from the dead. I receive the forgiveness of

my sins through the blood of Jesus. Take
out my old heart, Lord, and give me a new
heart and a new life. Make me born again.
I accept your love and grace to help me
follow you all the days of my life, in Jesus'
Name. Amen!"

Now listen. That is just the beginning.
God wants you to grow. He wants you to
move forward and live in His purpose for
your life. When we get born again, we start
a brand-new life. You don't have to live like
you used to live. But we all need help to live

out this new life in Christ. If you have just received Jesus as your Savior and Lord, contact our prayer center at 847-645-9700 and let us know. I want to help you.

Next Steps: Read the Bible and talk to God. God has a great plan for your life. He loves you and wants the best for you. You are His child now. You are in the family of God today. Your life will never be the same again!

Now thank Him for making you His child. And don't doubt! You are a child of

God right now! John 1:12 says, "To as many as received Him [Jesus], to them He gave the right to become sons and daughters of God."

Next, you should find a good Bible-believing church, where you can grow together with other believers and find your place in a spiritual home! **It is my pleasure to welcome you into the family of God!**